The Hillside Story

Thor Sorenson

FULL COURT PRESS
Duluth, MN 55811

Ten year old Thor and his dog "Coco"

Library of Congress Card Number: 99-06970

Published in association with Savage Press.

ISBN 1-886028-43-5

Swish Productions
Full Court Press

Aknowledgements

I would like to extend a heartfelt thank you
to those who contributed their time and support
to the development of this book, so it can be a
tool to touch the lives of others.

My best friend and beautiful wife Karen,
for all her support in my vision.

My mentor and father in the faith Lynn Kern,
for telling me that Jesus loves me.

My wonderful Mother for being so willing
to put her life on the pages of this story
so that others might find Jesus.

My earthly father who, seated in Heaven, looks on
with cheers of excitement.

My brothers and sisters for loving and supporting me
in this endeavor.

And to my beautiful church family
at Hermantown Community Church,
for catching the vision to touch our city
with the Good News of Jesus!

And to the following for their technical support
and encouragement:

Teresa Johnson	My secretary
Kristen Almer	Cover art
Jay Steinke	Photography
Taylor, Nancy & Bill	Cover picture
Ed Newman	Editing & design

Most of all, to my wonderful Lord Jesus.
May He receive all the glory!

Thor and Karen with daughter Kelcie and son Thor, just entering the ministry full time.

TABLE OF CONTENTS

PREFACE

I believe we can learn a lot from each other. In The Hillside Story, I'll be sharing my true life story with you. My desire is that you'll see that there's hope when all you see is despair, there's joy even through pain, and there really is a God who loves this lost and dying world.

Let this story speak to your heart. Then please share your own story with others.

This book is dedicated to all the hurting
people who need to see a way out of their pain.

Chapter 1

The Hillside

WHEN I WAS IN GRADE SCHOOL John F. Kennedy visited our town just a few blocks from my house. Through the large crowd I could hardly see him waving and smiling at everyone.

Yes, it was quite an eventful day to have the President of the United States come through the Hillside. These were the tumultuous 60's. Hippies, Hells Angels, and hallucinogenic drugs were hot items in the news along with landing the first man on the moon and listening to the Beatles on the Ed Sullivan show. The world seemed to be in an uproar. The Vietnam Conflict began taking over the headlines and the threat of nuclear war was always looming in the back of our minds. In spite of all this, I felt my neighborhood was a safe place to grow up. I never realized it was looked at in such disdain by others. I didn't know anything different.

Along with poverty, the crime rate was high in the Hillside area. Dysfunctional families were the norm. My neighborhood was probably like heaven compared to the Bronx in New York or the Inner City of Chicago. It wasn't the neighborhood that troubled me as much as my home life. I couldn't bear it.

U.S. News and World Report, in its October 17, 1994 issue, stated that the Duluth Central Hillside was ranked as the 5th worst white slum in America.

I remember walking through the Hillside hearing and seeing the fighting and abuse on a regular basis. It just seemed normal. Divorce, single parents, the children of drug addicts and alcoholics all seemed to have the same life style. It's a vicious circle leaving its victims with little or no hope. The problem is more severe now than ever before.

Just a month ago I was talking with a Duluth police officer. His beat was my old neighborhood in the Central Hillside. He stated that today it is worse than ever. "The kids I had problems with fifteen years ago in grade school I am having bigger problems with today as young adults. There is no hope for the Hillside," he said. As he made these remarks he also said he recently started wearing his bullet proof vest.

My heart hurt when he sounded so negative towards the Hillside. Another Central Hillside officer shared similar feelings. He said, "Thor, I hate to sound cynical, but there is no way these kids are going to change. There is no hope for them."

I disagree with this verdict. The following life story is proof that there is hope for inner city youth.

Chapter 2

Alcohol: My Dad's Best Friend

REMEMBER one of my college professors stating that anyone who is raised in a dysfunctional setting will have problems with dysfunction in life. If that is true I should be a basket case in some institution. I didn't agree with my professor then and I still don't.

I was raised in a home that was filled with all kinds of dysfunction. Alcohol abuse, suicide attempts, violence, fighting, poverty—we had it all. There were five children growing up in what looked like, from the outside, a normal family. My blue-collar dad was a hard working welder. Mom stayed at home with us kids, which was pretty good compared to many of our neighbors. Sadly, we never had nice things in our home. My mother had to beg dad simply to get money for school clothes or groceries. This frequently led to arguments because he said she spent too much. Tension almost always filled our home. Because of the way we lived I thought we were poor.

I shared a bedroom with my two younger twin brothers Henry and Paul. My two older sisters Paula and Joan shared another room. My parents occupied the third bedroom. We had a fairly nice home to live in and sometimes we actually had good times together. My Dad would take us camping and fishing on family vacations; but he also brought along his best friend. Yes, booze was my Dad's best friend. He didn't go anywhere without it!

I remember vividly the time I was packing for a camping trip while mom kept calling Malostins, the local pub, trying to get my dad to come home. "I'll be home real soon," he promised over and over again, until finally my mom sent me to get him. A passing squad car saw my father's inebriated condition and wouldn't allow him to get behind a wheel. I cried and begged the police to let my dad come home, but they said he was too drunk to drive. It turned out to be just one of many terrible scenes. Consequently, another vacation was ruined.

Dad worked out of town the majority of the time. Mom stayed at home taking care of us five kids. I recall the weekends dad would come back to Duluth. When he came home we'd greet him at the door, take his boots off and treat him like a king. My mother would make him special candlelight dinners and wait for his arrival. Unfortunately, he seldom came directly home. Instead, he'd stop for a few drinks with the guys. Mom would be patient and call the bar to tell him dinner was ready. "I'll be home in a few minutes," he promised, yet he seldom found his way home until after the bars closed. Over and over again he broke my mother's heart. Somehow he would get home, but the next morning he would have to go and hunt his car down. He never seemed to remember where he left it.

Almost every holiday and birthday was ruined because of my dad's drinking. When it was Christmas, my mother would cry because she couldn't buy us hardly anything. My dad needed his money for drinking and gambling. I remember my friends calling and asking what I got for Christmas and I was always embarrassed to answer because it was never much to speak of. Our birthday parties were likewise almost always ruined by my dad. My mother did her best to make them special but my dad would come home drunk, laughing loudly, totally humiliating us.

I love my dad, but that doesn't erase all the terrible memories that have haunted our family for years because of his drinking. My dad justified his lifestyle because his own father drank. I remember my Grandpa Thor saying, "Bob, you have to quit that drinking." "Ya, ya who are you to talk? You didn't quit until you were in your seventies," my dad would bellow. My dad continued to drink and it became his first love. The consuming power behind it was from the pit of hell.

Chapter 3

Midnight Terror

T WAS TWELVE O'CLOCK MIDNIGHT once again.
Almost every weekend at this time I'd begin to tremble
inside. When I got older I wouldn't even go home, it was so
intense. I'd lay awake in bed, dreading the moment I might hear
my parents stumbling up the stairs. My mother finally couldn't
take being alone at home all the time, so she joined my dad in the
bars. If you can't beat-'em join-'em, and that's what mom did.
However, mom couldn't function well at all under the influence of
alcohol. She was depressed already because of her life, and
alcohol is a depressant; the combination seemed to trigger a
bizarre chemical reaction. As a result, she'd go crazy.

"Go to hell," she would scream as I heard my parents opening the door.

"Now Janice, that's O.K.," dad would say, trying to console my mother. But he seldom succeeded in calming her. Crash, bang, boom, bang, the fighting would intensify for hours until finally, out of pure exhaustion, my mom would pass out. I savored this time of quiet, yet always feared with any noise that the fighting would erupt once more. In the morning the house looked like a war zone. Broken pieces of glass covered the floor, furniture turned on its side, and terror still filled the air for all five of us kids as we tip-toed around the house, cleaning the mess and trying not to wake our parents.

This was a typical weekend event at the Sorenson home while we were growing up. You'd think that sooner or later you would get used to the fighting and screaming and that it wouldn't scare or hurt you so much, but that fear and pain never seemed to subside. It's interesting that nothing was ever mentioned about the previous night of chaos.

My parents both continued to drink on the weekends while we fended for ourselves at home. As things got worse, I became more and more rebellious. My sisters tried to handle me but they couldn't. Although my twin brothers seemed to take it all in stride, I could see the fear in their young eyes. We felt helpless and didn't know what we could do to change things in our home. Things seemed hopeless.

Chapter **4**

God Please Help Us

SLEEPING IN BED ALONE was too frightening. When things really started to intensify at home, during the fighting, all five of us kids would huddle up together on one bed and try to console one another. It was so hard to hold the fear in. Parents shouldn't ever hurt each other because it terrifies their children.

I'll never forget the night mom was really screaming, swearing, and throwing things. As we huddled close to each other, I cried out in desperation to God. "Please help us dear God, we need you, please help." That's all I remember doing, crying out in desperation for God to help. But things just seemed to go from bad to worse. There didn't seem to be any way out for us.

Finally, the noise subsided, but the fear and terror loomed ever closer. We huddled together hoping and praying that the fighting was over for the night, when all at once we heard a horrendous scream, "I'm dying! I'm dying! Help me I'm dying!"

Terror shot through my body like a blast of lightning.

"Go see," one of us said.

"No, you go!"

Finally, we all ran together to the ugly scene. There, lying on her back in the middle of the dark gloomy room, my mother cried out again, "I'm dying, help, help, I'm dying."

"Please don't die, Mommy," I cried as I rubbed her sweat-covered forehead with my hand.

"We love you Mommy. Things will get better."

"No, no, I'm dying," she gasped. "Call my mother and tell her I'm dying."

I screamed at my sisters to call Grandma Helen in South Dakota. "Hurry!"

We scurried to find the number. My mother agonized on the floor, hyperventilating, fighting for every breath, babbling incoherently while the pupils of her glossy dark eyes dilated. My sisters held her down on the floor trying to calm her. My dad, as usual, was passed out, so it was up to us to take care of our 'dying' mother. This became our new family ritual.

Sometimes mom would pass out. Other times she became violent, trying desperately to harm herself. We ended up hiding knives, razor blades, medicines, even frying pans whenever she blacked out. On those occasions when we were able to reach Grandma Helen, my mother would eventually calm down. "I'm dying Momma," she'd say and Grandma, listening, would tell her that she loved her. Then my mother would calm down.

My mother needed that affirmation desperately. She had a terrible childhood. She had been taken away from her mother at a young age and shipped from one boarding home to the next. At the age of twelve she had to start taking care of herself. She went back home from time to time while pain and sorrow followed her all the way. When she was a young teen she was raped and forced by her family to have a back street abortion. The guilt and shame haunted my mother for years.

What actually happened is that my mother was asked out on a blind date. She was only fourteen years old at the time. Back in the forties there wasn't too much to do for entertainment, but young people still enjoyed the music and dances of the day. After the date on the way home she was raped by this restless, ruthless adolescent. A few months later she finally told her sister what happened. She was too ashamed to tell anyone at first, however after she found out she was pregnant she had no other alternative.

Her sister consoled her yet went directly to their mother. When my grandmother found out about my mother's situation she brought her to a doctor who performed the illegal abortion. This hideous act caused deep emotional hurt in my beautiful mother for years to come.

You'd think that one such crime would be enough for a young girl to experience, but not so for my dear mother. A few years later she moved to Seattle, Washington. Only sixteen at the time, she was working hard to take care of herself. One night after work, while walking to her apartment three men jumped out of a dark alley and forced my mother into an abandoned building. Her life was spared but that was all she escaped with. There in that dark hell hole three men robbed her of every bit of self-esteem she had left in her young life. At knife point they forced my mother to perform all kinds of degrading sexual acts while hankering over their filthy pornography. After these reprobates finished repeatedly raping my mother they finally let her go.

Though my mother kept this dark secret to herself, it haunted her for decades to come. My mother is close to seventy years old and as recent as a year ago she woke up out of her sleep in a cold sweat horrified from another nightmare out of her past.

My mother met dad at a bar in Sioux Falls, South Dakota. Dad was in Sioux Falls on a boiler job and after work he and his friends stopped by the local bars to have a few drinks. It was there he spotted the beautiful woman he eventually married. From Sioux Falls they moved to Duluth.

For mother, dad was her knight in shining armor, taking her away on his white horse. It had been her dream to have a loving husband and a beautiful family. She did everything humanly possible to bring that dream to pass.

In many ways she became involved with our neighborhood. For example, she served as a den mother, a great one at that. People still stop me on the street to ask how Mom's doing; they all loved her. At one point she became very religious and even tried to tell us kids about Jesus. We never wanted to listen. We went to church on holidays as a family, but that was about all. It was holiday Christianity. My dad boasted in having his religion, but he never seemed to practice it.

Yes, my mother had a dream to have a nice family with a husband to love and share her life with. She tried her best, yet her dream ended tragically, like so many do. There seemed to be little or no hope. Now, instead of just her nightmare, it was our nightmare, too.

Chapter 5

Mommie Please Don't Die

FTER THE FIRST EPISODE of my mother crying out
that she was dying I feared a repeat of that scene more
than any other. Yet it seemed inevitable, because of the way my
parents were living. During the week when my dad was gone
things seemed fairly normal, but the weekends came all too quick.

Worst of all, we had no one to talk to about our dilemma.
We were too embarrassed to tell our friends and too scared to tell
our relatives. Mom used to say we'd get taken away if we told. It
was our private business, no one else's. Until things got really bad,
we appeared to be a fairly normal family.

I'll never forget the fear that gripped me when my mother
was so very desperate for help. There was a weekend when it

happened again. The fighting, the yelling, the swearing. The horrifying anxiety of feeling all alone in the storm. There I was— lying in bed, eyes wide open, heart pounding through the covers—just waiting and hoping it would go away. It was as if death were pounding at our door. Then it happened, the screech. "I'm dying, I'm dying," echoed through the house.

Would she die this time or was it another false alarm? All of us kids gathered together for support, working our way down the long dark hall to the stairs. Once again the demonic screeching, "I'm dying," chilled our bones. We were paralyzed with fear.

Finally we all ran together to the living room to find our mother lying there gasping for air. We threw our arms around her and screamed, "Don't die, Mommie, please don't die."

She pushed us away and yelled again, "Help, help, I'm dying! Call my mom! I'm dying."

We couldn't get through and panic filled the air. My mother crawled to the bathroom and shut the door. Such a long period of silence followed that it seemed something must be wrong. We tried to force the door open but couldn't get it ajar.

"Mom, are you O.K.?" we cried.

Nothing but silence. Finally we broke through to find my mother lying on the floor with an empty bottle of aspirin and a razor blade in her hand. I dropped to my knees in desperation and tried to grab the razor blade. She wouldn't let go, staring through me like a demon.

"Get out of here," she growled.

"No, mom. Give me the razor blade," I cried.

I couldn't get it from her. She was so strong and wouldn't let go. I held her wrists apart, as she was trying to cut them. (I never knew it at the time but my mother attempted to take her life in the same manner when I was a young child.) Finally, my sisters called for help. The minutes we waited seemed like hours. Then the police and paramedics arrived and tried to talk with my mom. She tried to get away, but finally fell to the floor.

"Don't hurt my mother," I cried.

"We won't. We're just helping," they reassured me.

They put a straight jacket around my mother and tightened the straps. It looked terrible and I thought she was in pain.

"Let her go," I cried. The red light of the ambulance circled the Hillside neighborhood as they took my mother away. We were alone, scared and helpless. That night we went back to bed not knowing what tomorrow would bring.

Chapter 6

It's Me, Thor

E COULDN'T SEE OUR MOTHER the next day. The days ran into weeks before we finally were able to go to the hospital. The hospital psychiatric ward was a scary place. Sterile and cold, it made me feel awkward and uncomfortable. No one ever counselled or advised us on how to act, what to say, or what to expect. We hardly dared discuss it. "Your mom is in a deep depression," I remember being told, "but you can go in the room and see her."

I'll never forget the dead silence as I inched my way closer and closer. Finally, I was standing face to face with my dear mother.

"Hi, Mom," I said.

Silence.

"Hi, Mommie," I said again. Still she didn't respond.

Was she mad at me? Was I at fault? I was only eleven years old and had no one to turn to. All these feelings flooded my mind till finally I yelled, "It's me, Thor! Don't you know me? Talk to me, Mom!"

All she did was gaze off in a blank stare at the wall in front of us. It was like she wasn't there at all.

I left the hospital feeling all alone, scared, angry and hurt. I began to take my frustration out on others, especially my sisters and my brothers, yelling, fighting, threatening to run away. I began to do whatever it took to get attention.

I hated my family, my school, and my life. Everything seemed to be dark and dismal around me. I was sent to the principal continuously for getting into fights or talking disrespect-fully to my teachers. One of the older teens in the neighborhood had a habit of beating up on the younger kids. He started doing it to some kids during my rebellious rampage. I told him to stop it. He challenged me to make him. I flew at him with all my pent up anger and threw him to the ground. I punched him continually with furious blows to his body until his twenty year old brother came to his rescue.

My anger was getting out of control. Two other hoods in

the Hillside beat up one of my friends pretty bad. I thought it was my responsibility to vindicate my friend. I'll never forget my friend's look when these two thugs knelt down on their knees on First Avenue East as I made them apologize to my friend and promise to never hurt him again.

Yes, I thought I was a big tough guy. In reality, I was a hurting young boy screaming with all my heart for someone to rescue me from my pain.

At last my mother came home. She seemed a little different, and things even seemed to get better for awhile. My dad was a little more sensitive to my mother and spent more time at home until my mother got back to normal. I guess I didn't know what normal was. The house was always dark now. Mother kept all the curtains closed so even on nice days it was dark and gloomy. She also locked herself away in her bedroom for long periods at a time.

I began to get into a lot of trouble at school. Because I was always fighting, my teachers were continually sending me to the office to talk with the guidance counselor, Mr. Rindahl. He was a nice man. Maybe down deep that is why I kept getting into trouble. I liked talking to him. He would sit me down and lecture a little and then he would ask if he could read me a few verses from his black Bible. "Sure," I said, thinking *anything to stay out of class*. He seemed so sincere in his job. I think he really cared for me. I could sense something real about him. I'd behave better for the rest of the day, but it wouldn't be long before I was in trouble once again.

I wanted my mother to buy me a black leather jacket and black boots. I wanted to dye my blonde hair black too, but she wouldn't let me.

The nice friends I had wouldn't come to my house because their parents told them I was a hood. That's what we used to call troublemakers back then. It hurt my feelings. Deep down I wanted to change, but I didn't know how.

Chapter 7

Can I Play?

ALL OF THE KIDS I LIKED PLAYED BASKETBALL, so I thought I would try it myself. It was like putting a square peg in a round hole. I didn't seem to fit with the guys, but I kept trying.

Eventually the guys started a sixth grade team and I wanted to be on it. They said they would have to vote to see whether or not I could play. After a long discussion one of the guys came over to me and said it was a very close vote, "but we're going to let you play." Except for the close vote part I felt pretty good to be a part of something.

I began to practice basketball non-stop. I remember one of

our first games I got to play in. The action on the floor was intense. I got the ball for the first time and thought of one thing only, I was going to take the ball to the hoop and score. I faked one way and took off in the other. I seemed to be alone on the court. I heard the yelling in the background, but there was no one for half the distance of the basketball court in front of me. I was on the way to prove myself to the team as a player. I dribbled down the court and flew up towards the rim, the ball careening off the board and through the hoop. Yes, 2 points! I scored! I turned back to run down the court only to see people laughing. "What did I do?" I asked. " You scored for them, Sorenson, not us." Ouch! Wow, did I feel stupid. I scored for the wrong team. Oh well, they got over it and so did I.

At our school I was probably the least likely to succeed at basketball or for that matter anything. But I kept trying to improve. It really helped me to have something to occupy my time other than my problems. Basketball, baseball, and football became fun pastimes for me with my new found friends. It felt so good to be a part of something and to have special friends to talk with and to do good things together. I'm not sure what direction my life might have taken if those boys would have told me I couldn't play on their team.

Chapter 8

Black & Blue

OST FAMILIES that have problems with alcohol or drugs reap many side effects as a result. As I shared before, I really believe I had two special parents. I loved them dearly, however, they desperately needed help. My mother always kissed us and hugged us to pieces when she could catch us. She told us how much she loved us and we believed it. I think that's what made it so hard to see her suffer. My dad was a good man, too. We loved and respected him, but with dad we'd never hear the words "I love you" come out of his mouth. He was a very quiet and intelligent person. But little by little his addiction to alcohol was destroying him and his family.

One of the side effects of alcohol was abuse. Verbal and

physical abuse are cousins to drugs and alcohol. When my dad was drunk he would tell my mother all kinds of degrading things that wounded her spirit. He would do the same to us. It was a terrible thing to experience, but the abuse went beyond words alone. After one beating I was so bruised that I had to lie to my grandparents when they came to visit. I was told to tell them that I had fallen on my bike and hurt myself. After the beating I had to sit in the back seat of the car while my parents drove to pick up my sisters who had been swimming at Twin Ponds. When my sisters got in the car they recall being shocked.

"You looked like you had been in a car accident," they have since told me. "We both asked in shock, 'What happened to Thor?' We were told to shut up. We never knew what had happened to our little brother Thor. It was never discussed, just like many other things in our home life. We felt so bad for you as you curled up in a ball looking so scared and all alone, but there was nothing we could do for you."

I was getting so rebellious my parents had a hard time handling me. Of course this experience is not unique to my home alone. It's happening in every city of America today. Rich and poor alike, people are being abused and hurt because of their terrible addictions and pent up problems.

My parents weren't the only ones who had a hard time

controlling me. At school I would drive most of my teachers to the point of exhaustion. Many times my teachers would spank me, throw me against a wall, or pull my hair to get me to behave. Nothing seemed to help.

We went to church while my mom and dad stayed at home with hangovers. While in Sunday school I cursed at my teachers and caused all kinds of confusion. I couldn't stand seeing all the hypocrisy of religion. One class would get confirmed and you would hardly ever see them again after confirmation, except for a few religious holidays of the year. I continued going to church with my sisters for awhile and finally stopped that, too. I didn't realize until recently that the church people had asked my sister not to bring me to church anymore unless I attended with my parents, and that very seldom happened.

Things continued to disintegrate in our home life. My mom tried tirelessly to get my dad to stop drinking, but to no avail. Again mom started drinking with dad and the fear once more gripped our home.

Our challenge was no longer just stopping our mother from suicide attempts or episodes of near death experiences. We were trying to keep her from leaving home. She would tell us we didn't love her and that we loved our dad. "You can have your dad," she'd say. Then she'd pack her suitcase and say she was going to leave us for good. This was our greatest fear. We'd cry out and beg her to stay till finally she would calm down and listen to us. Once we had reaffirmed our love for our mother, things would go back to normal for a little while.

Chapter 9

Daddy Please Come Back

N THE FALL OF 1967 my basketball aspirations were flying high. There was a church down the street from our house that allowed Hillside kids to come and use their gym. That gym at First Presbyterian Church kept many of us off the streets at a young age.

There was a kid there who started on the 9th grade team that always beat me playing one on one. I would go home and dream of beating him and taking his spot someday on the varsity team at Central High School.

That fall I asked my dad for a basketball hoop and backboard. I'll never forget that homemade set up. It wasn't pretty, but it was from my dad and that meant the world to me. I played on that court all fall and right through the winter of 1967-68. I shoveled off the court and practiced left hand lay-ups, then free-throws, then my jump shot. Over and over again I would work out.

The next summer I was at the church gym practicing. The kid I wanted to eventually replace on the High School team walked in to the gym. I asked if he wanted to play a game of one-on-one. Sure, he said with a major attitude. I said, "You take it first." He did and he scored. I scored next and then I stole the ball. I was in control and I beat him the first game. He asked for another and I said sure, this time I felt like I had total control. I beat him again. Two in a row and I felt great. He never asked me to play again. I eventually took his posititon on the varsity team. He ended up quitting shortly after that summer contest.

One of the reasons I played basketball was to get out of the house and to make friends. When I finally started having some success, a stunning event took place in our family.

I knew things weren't good between mom and dad, however I was glad my parents were still together. Mom intimated now and then that she couldn't take anymore and she threatened to leave our home. Actually, she packed her bags quite a few times, only to have the five of us kids begging, crying, and pleading with her to stay home with us. She would finally calm down, unpack her bags and for a period of time life would resume some form of normalcy again.

I guess down deep I knew that divorce was inevitable, but I never dreamed it would hurt so much. It seems so right to have a mom and dad that live together under the same roof, and there is a real sense of security just knowing that they are together. Unfortunately, today in our society, it's no longer the norm to have a home that has not been divided by divorce.

What a totally depressing day it was when mom quit yelling and fighting. I know that sounds ironic, but when the fighting quit I knew my mother had given up. Actually, she had no fight left in her. She was devastated. Inside I knew that the talk and threats of divorce would eventually become a reality. It was a fear deep inside me and nobody could ease the pain.

As I was walking home from school I pondered the effects a divorce would have on our family. I'll never forget that dark day. It became my black Friday. I climbed up the steps and walked into the house. There was dead silence; nobody would say anything.

"Where's Dad?" I asked.

"Upstairs," Mom said sharply.

I ran upstairs to say "hi" to my dad. When I opened his bedroom door I was shocked. The thing I feared for years was coming true. I saw my dad leaning over his bed packing his brown cardboard suitcase. This time, though, he wasn't packing to go out of town for work. He was leaving our home for good.

As I looked closely at my dad's face, I saw something I had never seen before in my dad. I saw fear and deep remorse, but it was too late. All those hurts had built a wall far too high to tear down.

"Daddy don't leave. Stay here. You paid for this house. You don't have to leave."

"Yes, I do son," my dad said quietly. "You be a good boy for your mother. She's a wonderful lady."

I ran downstairs yelling at the top of my lungs. "You can't make daddy leave us. Why are you doing this to our family, Mom?"

I was very angry towards my mother. Isn't it sad how the victim is so often the party that receives the blame. My mother tried to hug and console me, but I would have none of it. I ran upstairs again to see my dad. As I opened the door I witnessed something I had never seen before and would never see again. My dad was leaning over his suitcase with tears streaming down his cheeks. I hugged my dad and didn't want to let go, but he sat me aside and left the room.

I followed him to his '62 Ford wagon but he drove off

without me. The pain I felt inside was indescribable. Why didn't someone tell my parents how much it would hurt all of us and that the pain would stay with us for years? There was no one available to help us. It was too late.

My pain turned into hate and aggression. I continued getting into trouble at home and in school. Mother tried her best to be a good mother and she tried to be a father to us, too. No matter how hard she tried, she couldn't fill the void that was formed after my dad left home.

Mom was very creative. I wanted a weight set, but there was no money to buy such things in our home. My mother improvised. She took coffee cans and an old broomstick, mixed cement by hand and made me the neatest weight set a boy could ever dream of.

I loved All-Star Wrestling. It was one of my favorite pastimes to go to the Duluth Arena with Grandpa Thor and watch the Crusher take on Mad-Dog-Vashan, or The Man with the Iron Stomach, or Reggie Park take on the honorable Kenny Yates. My favorite must have been Doctor X alias the Masked Man, with his devastating figure four leg lock. I'll never forget the night Mad Dog tore a chunk out of the Alaskans ear and spit it towards my grandfather and I.

"Grandpa," I said, "this must be fake."

"What, what's that you say? This is as real a fight as you'll ever find," he shouted.

So then I knew what I would be when I grew up: an All-Star Wrestler.

How on earth could a single mom try to fulfill that fantasy for her 12 year old son? Mom once again displayed her love for me by putting her creative mind to action. She built a 12' X 12' wrestling ring right in our front yard. We had kids from all over the Hillside throwing body slams in that special homemade ring. Tagteam matches were my favorite. We would jump off the top ropes and almost kill each other. Now I knew this wasn't a circus. All-Star Wrestling was the real thing.

After dad left home things were a little better, but that didn't last for long. I still missed my dad and longed for his attention. The only place I could visit him was downtown at one of the local bars. I'd sit and play cards with the guys and my dad just so I could be by him. The more I frequented the bars, the more I began to detest everything about them. The gambling, flirting, yelling, backbiting, even the smell made me sick; but there was nothing I could do. My dad was addicted to alcohol and there didn't seem to be a way out for any of us.

My mother would always accuse me of loving my dad more than I loved her. This wasn't true at all. I have always loved my mother very much, but I was angry that she made dad leave home. A boy really needs a dad to look up to and I wanted to be around my dad as much as I could.

One of the devastating effects of divorce is that it sometimes causes children to choose between parents, even if the parents are not consciously trying to cause division.

Chapter 10

Mom and the Murderer

FTER MY DAD WAS OUT OF THE PICTURE my mother soon began going back to the bars. I couldn't understand why she would go back to the very thing that caused our family to go through such trauma and heartache. Mom was lonely, hurting, and broke. All she had to look forward to after work was coming home to more work. I have a real love and respect for single parents. It's no picnic doing it all alone.

At first my mother would just go to the bars to have some adult conversation, but it wasn't long before she started drinking to ease the pain and forget her problems for a little while. I was afraid that we would see my mother regress to the point of being suicidal and desperate once again. That did not take place right away, but something just as bad did. Mom started bringing boy-friends home with her from the bars. I never gave them a chance. They tried to be mister nice guy to me, but I hated and despised them. I believe that most children in single parent families have a hard time seeing another person come in and try to take the place of their parent. In most situations that I have personally encoun-tered, it has proven to be so.

The guys my mother were dating were not close to being on par with my dad. These men didn't have good jobs, they were stupid, they were drunks and reprobates and some had bad tempers. I remember at times they would try to win my friendship by throwing the baseball or shooting baskets, but I was too hard-ened to get close to anyone.

I'll never forget the night the yelling started in our home once again. This time my dad was not the culprit. It was my mom's boyfriend who was causing the terror in our home. I heard my mother yelling, "Stop it, don't do that, leave me alone now," but the jerk wouldn't listen to her.

I stormed down the stairs ready to fight. "Get out of the house right now!" I shouted.

He wouldn't listen.

I threatened him, "Get out of here or I'll tear your head off."

"Do you think you're big enough and strong enough to do that?" he gloated.

"I know I am," I snarled as I tried to flex my 120 pound frame.

I don't think I intimidated him at all but he finally got his jacket on and headed towards the door. He turned around and said, "When you're big enough I'll let you try me."

I couldn't wait to get big enough. On the next encounter I had with this guy, I decided to use my brains and make up for my present lack of muscle power. My mom was trying to beat the guy off, but again he wouldn't listen and he didn't let up. I ran to the phone and called the Duluth Police and they were there in a flash. Two of the policemen grabbed the man and pulled him toward the door. I'll never forget my mother's tears and fear as the man was leaving or his lying words as he was being put into the squad car,. "I love you, honey... I'll always love you... I'll be back."

Those words haunted me. "I love you, I'll be back." What did this guy, who was hurting my mother, know about love? I dreaded the day I would see him in my house again. The police only held him for a short time. Because my mother wouldn't press charges he was free.

Before long he was back visiting my mother. He was nice to her at times and so she enjoyed his companionship. She even talked about getting married to him. I said I'd leave if she ever married him. The events that were about to transpire alleviated my fears for some time.

I had a close friend that played basketball with me who lived in a very similar environment. His father was an alcoholic, too. When his father was real drunk, my friend would come and stay at my house and when things were tough for me at home I would run over to his home. My friend was black, consequently his dad warned him not to trust whites. It never mattered to my friend or I what color we were. We just liked each other and had a lot in common. One night when my friend and I, along with my sister, were watching TV together, the house was suddenly filled with police officers. They scared us half to death. Armed with 12 gauge shotguns, they searched the house.

"What are you doing?" I asked.

"Just a routine check," they replied.

Then they asked where my mom was. I said she was at work and should be home soon. They called her and picked her up at work. When she arrived home they began to question her about her boyfriend. She said she hadn't seen him lately but she expected a call sooner or later. Then they prepared to trace his incoming call. They finally said they were after him for shooting a man that night. My mother looked devastated. They set up their headquarters in our home. After we waited for hours in dead silence, the phone rang. It was him. They coached her into keeping him on the phone long enough to trace the call and all at once they said, "We've got him." She hung up the phone and it was over. He never entered our house again. He ended up going to prison for murder.

Things were never too quiet in the Hillside and much of the activity seemed to be concentrated at our house.

Chapter 11

Hillside Basketball

BASKETBALL IN THE HILLSIDE was a big thing back in the '60's & '70's. It's still one of the favorite sports for young people in the Central School District. I mentioned previously that one of my main goals in life was to play on Central's Varsity basketball team. What I didn't realize was just how much basketball would be used in changing my life.

If you were to walk in the Central High School gym, you would see the tremendous legacy that has been a part of Duluth's pride. There, mounted high on the gymnasium walls, are plaques reminding the students and players who enter of their great heritage. State champs once, twice, three, four times. Third place, runner up, the list goes on as you scan the walls.

This was almost every kid's dream in the Hillside, to be a part of something so special.

In the 7th grade my group was labeled the gym rats. They couldn't get us to leave. Slithering our slender bodies through the metal gates we'd sneak into the gym when only the custodian was there. He caught us many times, but saw that our motives were good and finally just said, "Come on in, I'll turn the lights on for you boys anytime."

The senior high coaches, Jim Hastings, Tom Brayden and Sherm Moe, heard of our zeal. They were so impressed that the head coach decided he would meet with us in the gym for practice everyday before school started. That spring, when the team took 3rd place at the State Tournament, Duluth had a huge homecoming for their high school heroes. I'll never forget the words of Coach Hastings at that rally. "Central Basketball has a great tradition of success," he said. "We are already looking forward to our 7th grade gym rats taking up the torch."

Wow, did that make our day! He meant it, too. He felt we would be one of the better teams at Central.

We couldn't get enough gym time. We played every chance we could. Then we heard of another gym where we could play ball. First Pres was straight down the hill from my house, just a few blocks from beautiful Lake Superior. This wasn't the church any of us Hillside kids belonged to, though most of us didn't really belong anywhere. It didn't seem to matter, however, to the people at the church. They let us come and play basketball from morning to evening. We would actually bring our brown bag lunches and stay all day.

Some people have a hard time believing in a God that really loves and cares for us. I was that way. But at that little church gym I met a young man who helped me take a closer look. It was the month of July, 1968. Almost thirteen and going into the 8th grade, I was playing ball with a few friends when this college guy, Lynn Kern, asked if he could play ball with us. Sure, we said a little hesitantly, not knowing who he was. We played for an hour or so and then sat down for a pop. He asked us if we would like to come to a Bible study at the church later that evening. "A Bible study? Ya, right, no way," I shouted back sarcastically. Why should I go to a Bible study? My parents used to make me go to church on Sundays while they stayed in bed with hangovers. I didn't want anything to do with a Bible study.

"We'll play basketball first," he said.

Now that caught my attention. "OK, I'll come."

The only reason I went was because it was another chance to improve my basketball skills. We had fun that night playing ball and the Bible study wasn't as bad as I thought it would be.

This guy actually talked on our level. He invited us back the next night to do the same thing. We jumped at the chance. The next night I began asking Lynn a lot of questions about the Bible and about life. He was very patient and tried his best to field the questions. Again, he invited us to come back the next night. "Sure, this is kinda fun," I said.

The next night was the most memorable night of my life. It wasn't the basketball that drew me back that night. It was the Spirit of the Living God. We were all sitting down reading and discussing Paul's letter to the Romans. We were in Chapter 6. It was so interesting I couldn't stop asking questions. Poor Lynn, I wouldn't even let him finish one question before I asked another.

That chapter talked about being a slave to sin or a slave to God. I knew I was a slave to sin. My attitude towards my parents and teachers, or actually to anyone in authority, was out of line. I was challenged regarding my own rebellious Spirit. My language was vulgar. Mom would ask me to take the garbage out and immediately I would argue. Finally, reluctantly, while cuss words flew from my mouth, I would take it out. Yes, I was enslaved by sin. I tried to do good, but there seemed to be too much bitterness and resentment towards others. I had a hostile attitude towards others that seemed to engulf me. I couldn't rid myself of these feelings; it seemed hopeless.

Suddenly I felt an over-whelming urge to be free from my prison of sin. When we reached the last verse of Chapter 6, where it says "the wages (results) of sin is death but the gift of God is eternal life through Jesus Christ our Lord", that verse seemed to jump right off the page into my heart.

What happened next changed my life. I got up, left the table we were sitting at and knelt down by a chair. Nobody told me what to do. I wasn't pushed into making an emotional commitment to Christ. I just quietly, but sincerely, asked Jesus to set me free from my prison of sin. "Jesus," I asked, "please forgive me. I invite you to come into my heart. I want to serve you as my Lord and Savior." Wow! It was absolutely a miracle. I knew from that moment on that Jesus answered my simple prayer.

After meeting together that night, Lynn told me that he had prayed for five junior high school students to commit their lives to Jesus Christ by August 1, 1968. I never knew Lynn when he prayed that prayer, but God knew me.

I walked home with a heart filled with joy for the first time in my life. When I started up the stairs my mother came to the door.

"What happened to you?"she shouted. "Are you on drugs or what?"

"No, Mom, I'm not on drugs or alcohol. I found Jesus

tonight. I became a true Christian."

"Ya," she said. "It won't last. I tried it too when I was a kid."

"Yes it will, Mom!" I shouted joyously. Then I proceeded to tell her exactly word for word what happened. Afterwards, she just shrugged it off as some fad I would soon get over.

Years later my twin brothers shared with me that they had been listening as I told my mom what had happened that night. After hearing my story they went to their bedroom, got down on their knees and prayed that same simple prayer. They were 7 years old at the time. As for my sisters, however, that's a totally different story.

Chapter 12

Growing Pains

M Y SISTERS WERE WATCHING ME like two hawks. They heard my story, but were very skeptical of this born again experience that I was resounding throughout our home.

Many people have a hard time believing and receiving the born again message that Jesus taught in John Chapter 3. It's easier trusting in our religious traditions. Religious traditions however are one of the great traps that keep us from authentic Christianity.

In John Chapter 3 verse 3, Jesus told Nicodemous, who was one of the most religious men of his day, "You must be born again to have eternal life." In other words, Jesus was telling Nicodemous he needed the Spirit of God living within him. He needed a relationship with God, not just knowledge that God exists.

Nicodemous seemed confused. "How can I, being old, enter into my mother's womb and come out again?"

Jesus explained that this born again experience was a spiritual rebirth. A person must choose on his own volition to turn from a sinful lifestyle and follow Christ and His teaching, trusting Him alone for salvation. Nicodemous was uneasy about this new teaching. Finally, Jesus says in verse 7, "Nicodemous why do you marvel that I say you must be born again?" In other words why are you so surprised, or even confused, with my teaching? This is truly the way to the Father.

My sisters were the same way. They just couldn't understand this new phrase in our home. You must be born again. They, too, had religion, and thought that was enough. I'm sure I didn't present this wonderful message with an abundance of tact. I remember telling them they were sinners and they needed to change or they would go to hell. I really didn't use a lot of love when I shared it with my family.

As my sisters observed my new life in Christ they became very aware of the mistakes I made. And I made many. Sin is missing the mark. I missed that mark quite a bit in my new walk with Christ. I remember once when I was provoked over something, I said, "Oh ___." Yes, I used profanity. I blew it. I missed the mark and guess who was listening to me. You're right. Both of my sisters heard me swear. Boy, did they start rubbing it in. "Oh, what a Christian you are, Thor."

I couldn't take the criticism. I felt terrible. I said, "Ya, you're right," and I swore again and again at them. I walked away feeling very defeated. I went upstairs to my bedroom and knelt down by my bedside and prayed, "Oh God, please forgive me. I was a rotten example for you." Jesus always made me feel so accepted. I knew that He forgave me and I felt His love continually.

My sisters continued to observe everything I did and said. They were my personal tormentors. My mother had seen the difference, too, but she continued to go her way while I went mine. I'm not sure of the sequence of events, but God used a number of different people to touch my sisters' lives.

Billy Graham had a movie that came to the Duluth area. It was called The Restless Ones. It was at the movie The Restless Ones where my sisters responded to the challenge to come forward to receive Christ after the movie. This actually took place before my conversion. My sisters were very sincere about their conversion, but they had no support at all and consequently fell away. Nevertheless God's seeds were planted and He was at work in each of our lives in a very specific way.

Paula was the first to come back to Christ after she saw the miracle in my life. Then about two years later my sister Joan heard God say to her, "You act like a Christian, why don't you really become one." It was that day that she came back to Christ. Now we had five Christians living in our home. Although my twin brothers were the youngest in our home, their love for God was sincere and evident.

Lynn challenged us to invite our classmates to the Bible study that started back at the gym in July 1968 and it wasn't long before the group was so large that we had to start meeting in the gym. Soon over one hundred kids were coming to play basketball and trench ball. Then we would sing together and split into smaller groups for Bible study. The core group that God blessed Lynn with, including myself, were trained to lead the small group Bible studies. I was only in Junior High at the time. I didn't realize it then, but these were the building blocks preparing me for a life of service to God.

Lynn gave us many opportunities to share our faith. He had us write our personal testimonies down on paper. Then we would condense them and print small personal tracts to hand out to people on the street. Every Friday night we would go witnessing, either door to door or from one street corner to the next.

I'll never forget the first time I had an opportunity to preach in a church. We traveled north to the Iron Range. It was 30 below zero that night. In the old van we felt every bump in the road. I was nervous, yet I felt a burning desire to tell people what Jesus had done for me. After the singing stopped they finished sharing announcements and took the offering. I was next on the agenda. I walked up to the pulpit and turned towards the small congregation. "Let's pray," I said. "O God, help me tonight to share your love. Amen." As I looked out over the congregation, I began to feel excitement at being able to tell them what God had done for me. I opened my mouth and the first words I stammered were, "I'm not no Billy Graham, but God has changed me, too." Then the words began to flow.

God used many similar situations to help disciple and mold me into a minister of the Good News!

Our home life was still very unsettling, but now having brothers and sisters to pray with made it a lot easier. God was at work in our Hillside home, performing a miracle that would touch the lives of thousands of people in the years to follow.

Chapter **13**

State Champs

ILT CHAMBERLAIN WAS POSTING UP against Bill Russell while Jerry West was running the court. I remember watching basketball every chance I could on our old black & white RCA TV. While I was practicing, I would start the ten count 9, 8, 7... Sorenson has the ball, 6, 5... his team is down by 1 point... 4, 3... he fakes... 2, 1... dribbles, shoots, he scores. Central is going to the State Tournament once again. Yes, I would daydream at the gym about my basketball fantasies and at night I would go to sleep with my basketball. Shooting it softly off my finger tips, performing the art of perfect follow through.

I used all their names — Pistol Pete, Rick Mount — as I would release a shot from the top of the circle. They were our heroes as we were growing up. We'd continually pretend we were one of them as we played ball in the Hillside.

I was a sophomore in the fall of 1970. There was a battle to make the travelling team at Duluth Central High School. As a 10th grader I wasn't sure if I had a chance or not to play much varsity ball. At Central High you rarely see an underclassman getting much playing time. The majority of the upperclassmen that year went on to play college ball, and some played division one. That year our center actually went on to play pro ball.

Such was the scenario at Central. We were steadily winning ball games. When the team was up by 15 - 20 points, the coach would call on the tenth grade bombers to go in and keep the intensity up. It was fun being part of a great team. Although basketball was taking a lot of my time, I continued going to our youth group once a week and I wouldn't miss a Sunday church service. It was coming down to the end of the regular season. Now, they would have to pick the top fifteen players to be on the tournament roster. I wasn't sure if I would make the tournament team or not. I knew I had a good chance, but there were a lot of juniors and seniors playing ball that year, too. When the coach told us the final squad, I had made it. I was thrilled to finally be on the team I had dreamed about for years.

We had only lost one game all season, but anything could

happen in the tournament. We won all three games in our region. I'll never forget the championship game at the Duluth Arena. It was very similar to the movie Hoosiers.

My dad finally came to a ball game, but he came half drunk. It was always so frustrating to try and cover up for my dad. As I shared earlier, I loved my dad very much but it was so shameful to see him loud and obnoxious in public. Down deep I knew my parents were proud of me. I never once let bitterness destroy my relationship with my parents after I accepted Christ into my heart. I just prayed harder for them to become true Christians, too.

When the final buzzer sounded, I was on the floor with my hands raised high. We were on our way to the State Tournament in Minneapolis. The fans ran onto the court screaming, "We're #1, We're #1!"

The trip to Minneapolis was my first trip to the big city. I'll never forget gazing up at the Foshay Tower which at the time was the tallest building in Minnesota. Coach Brayden teased me and said I was just a country boy. We stayed at the Curtis Hotel and played our games at the Minnesota Gophers Gymnasium Williams Arena. We stood in awe as we walked out on the court. It seemed gigantic! We won our first game and enjoyed seeing our pictures in the Star Tribune the next day. "Duluth Central is the favorite for this year's tournament," the newspapers said. The coach reminded us not to let the papers go to our heads. Finally, after winning our first two games, we ended up in the championship game against a strong Anoka team. When we won the Double A Championship, the place went wild.

1970 was the first year we had a two class system, so we came back the next week to play the Single A Champion Melrose. It was a great game and a wonderful experience. We won the game and ended our season as the Minnesota State Basketball Champions.

I will never forget what our coaches engrained in our heads at Duluth Central. They said, "You're learning about life out here on the court. It's not just basketball. It's principles you will need the rest of your life."

They were absolutely right. Discipline, attitude, coachability, perseverance, sportsmanship, the list goes on and on. We were learning that sometimes life isn't easy. There might be a bad call by the ref in a game and in life there may seem to be some unfair calls too. Maybe life will seem like a double overtime game and you're losing. The key is to keep the right attitude. (Don't ever give up and learn to bounce back.)

I could never have bounced back in life without Christ. Jesus helped me to put my trust in Him no matter what. My close friend made the All State Team and at the tournament he broke all kinds of records, yet he said, "Thor, I feel empty inside." I told him that the void could only be filled by Christ. I offered to pray with him, but he wasn't willing to totally surrender to Christ.

I have a plaque that was given to me that says, "Let Jesus be your coach and you'll be a winner." A true Christian must be willing to follow Christ's instructions given to us in the Bible.

Chapter 14

Prostitutes and Angels

HERE IS A LOT OF TALK about angels in our society today. People of all backgrounds share similar experiences of the supernatural. I guess I never doubted the existence of angels. I just didn't give it much thought. The Bible tells us that God gives us angels to help us and minister to us. In one place it actually says we should be careful how we treat strangers, because it's possible we could actually be having an encounter with an angel without knowing it.

Although I believed in angels, I would not have dreamed that God would use one to answer my most fervent prayer, my mother's conversion to Christ. My mother is one of the dearest and most important people in my life. It devastated me to see her on a downhill skid after she divorced my dad.

She had to go to work to help support her five children. My mom had always been a hard worker and she taught us the importance of having a good work ethic. I'll never forget her work at home. We might have been poor, but we were always clean. She taught us the importance of taking pride in working to keep our house and yard looking nice even though we didn't have new things. Mom started getting ahead just a little. But then my dad was laid off, and her child support came to a halt. Mom couldn't support us on her menial income and she didn't know where to turn.

Looking back on our family situation gives me a deep respect and concern for single parents. It's a continual battle in every way — financial, disciplinary and school functions. It's demanding enough for two parents. I can see how my mother came to the point of desperation and exhaustion in her life. She tried to be a good mother, provider, supporter, she even tried to take the place of a father, but she couldn't see her way out.

I had been praying for my mother to give her life to Christ. Lynn Kern showed me the importance of bringing my problems to the Lord in prayer. He told me Jesus was concerned about every facet of my life.

We started a prayer list together after my conversion in the summer of 1968. I never imagined God would take so long to answer my prayers. My first prayer request was for my Mother to become a true Christian. It actually seemed like an eternity waiting for her conversion, but I continued to pray and believe that God heard my prayers. Lynn encouraged me to be patient and keep praying. It actually got worse rather than better. Mom was going downhill fast.

Norman's Bar was one of the hellholes my parents were accustomed to hiding out in. Because my mother was experiencing financial tension and loneliness she continued to ease the pain and worry by having a few drinks. My mother wasn't an alcoholic, she was just a lonely, hurting, desperate single parent looking for help. There were other people in similar situations that were her so-called friends. Two years after I began praying my mother was sitting at Norman's Bar sharing her problems with two women. They shared with her a quick way out of her financial distress.

"Janice," they said, "you can make good money by becoming a prostitute with us. It will solve all your problems immediately."

As she was giving this some serious thought she heard a voice say, "Janice, go home. Your children love you and need you."

She turned to the man next to her at the bar, hit him and

yelled, "Don't ever tell me to go home to my kids. I'm a good mother and it's none of your business where I am."

The man looked very surprised and calmly replied, "I didn't say anything to you."

"Yes you did," she argued.

But he adamantly denied saying anything.

Three times she heard the same thing. As she sat on that bar stool the words raced through her mind, "Go home to your children."

"Who said that?" she pondered. Finally, after thanking the women for their offer, she said, "I'm sorry, but I have to go home to my children." She called a cab and went home, still wondering where the words "go home to your children" came from. What she did not realize at the time was that they hadn't come from anyone on earth. God had sent an angel to whisper those words into her heart that dark and desperate night.

Yes, God heard my prayer, and He was faithful in His timing to answer the desperate cry of my heart. When my mother walked into the house that night I wasn't home, but my sister was there to greet her.

"What's wrong, Mom?"

"Nothing," she said. "I don't know what's going on. I guess I'm just supposed to be home," she cried.

Mom went upstairs, fell to her knees and cried out to Jesus to forgive her sins and come into her life.

God answered her prayer and set her free from her sin and fear. Now my mother had new hope. She was a new person and things at home began to change, including a completely different atmosphere. For the first time, peace and love began to reign in our home.

In Billy Graham's book, Angels, there are many beautiful examples of angelic visitation providing comfort, direction, protection, and many other benefits in our lives. The Bible tells us not to harden our hearts, but rather to listen and obey His voice. Today is the day of salvation. There is no promise that tomorrow will come for you or me. I am so thankful that God heard my prayer and rescued my Mother from her despair.

My mother's encounter with God began a permanent transformation in her life. Mom started attending church with all of us kids. It was so beautiful to be in church together as a family. Now, there was only one left out of seven members in my immediate family who had not become a true Christian. My Father didn't have a chance, with all six of us praying fervently for his salvation.

Chapter 15

I Love the Number Seven

WO YEARS SEEMED LIKE AN ETERNITY to wait for the salvation and transformation of my mother's life. I never dreamed it would take 24 years before my dad would finally surrender his life to the Lordship of Jesus Christ and experience God's wonderful grace.

The years seemed to fly by. It was my senior year in High School, and our home had finally become a nice place to live. We still had our struggles, but now we knew how to handle conflict and problems from a Biblical perspective. One day when we were fighting and bickering over some trivial things mom sat us down and told us that we were not acting like Christians. She said, "Forgiveness and patience are needed in our home, not quarreling." She made us get our Bibles and turn to the portion in John 13 where Jesus washed His disciples' feet. In verse 14 of that same chapter Jesus says, "Now that I have washed your feet I want you to remember to do the same for each other." Then my Mother said, "We are going to obey the Lord and wash each others' feet. Take off your shoes."

Now, before you hear the rest of this episode of my life I have to give you a little background. I hate feet. I couldn't even stand to look at my sister's feet, let alone touch them. The thought of washing those ugly toes made me sick. You see, my sisters used to sit next to me on the couch and little by little they would ease those ugly toes right on my body. Maybe it was my reaction that compelled them to be pests. Nevertheless, they did it all the time. Now imagine that yellow, hard, pungent, birds beak, implanted on a baby toe. Yes, this was the monster that haunted me throughout my childhood. Now I was being told to fetch a bucket of warm water and wash my sisters' feet. This had to be the ultimate test of my love for the Lord.

After the ceremony was over, there seemed to be a genuine sense of love and forgiveness that filled the room. My mother had shown me the importance of practicing, not just speaking, the words of Christ.

I mentioned before that our youth group was growing

continually. Lynn Kern was teaching Junior High students in the public schools. He had also "kidnapped" my oldest sister Paula. They got married on August 15, 1970. They allowed our youth group to meet in their home because the other building was no longer available. It was on one special night at one of these youth meetings that I realized a girl named Karen liked me. I had noticed her before in the eighth grade at Washington Junior High School, but it took me a few years to catch on to the fact that she was interested in me. She'd trip me in the halls once in a while, but I thought it was because she was clumsy. We dated off and on throughout high school. I knew I loved her and I wanted to marry her, but it wasn't going to be that easy.

One Friday in October of 1972 she decided to dump me. It was the same night my Volkswagen Bug went up in flames coming home from our homecoming football game. I asked her what was wrong, but she said she would tell me another time.

I said, "Go ahead and tell me now."

"Well," she said, "I just want to be friends."

My heart sank. I was devastated. She continued to come to youth group, but now it was different. She was dating other guys. I didn't know you could hurt so much on the inside. Now I could understand in part how my parents felt after their divorce. The pain is extreme and so hard to bear. The sad thing is that everybody involved in a divorce experiences the pain.

My dad continued to cover up his pain with alcohol. His drinking got worse. I had to go see him at the bars if I was going to see him at all. I would try to get there before he was too drunk to carry on a conversation. I loved my dad and honored him as my father, regardless of his condition.

After high school graduation, I felt God was calling me into full-time service. I had attended a seminar called Y.E.S. 73 (Youth Evangelism Seminar) put on by the Billy Graham team. While I was there learning how to share my faith more effectively, God was confirming His call on my life. At the seminar the Billy Graham team sent us out into the St. Paul area to witness to the neighborhood and invite them out to the evening crusade. When all the bus loads returned, they asked us what had happened during the outreach time. There were over 500 teens that went out evangelizing that day. We listened to many testimonies about our day, mine being one of them. I shared how God allowed me to pray with four people to receive Christ as their personal Savior. What a beautiful experience.

I didn't realize that they were going to pick five of us to go up on stage that night with Billy Graham and share with the crowd what happened that day. I was one of the five chosen. It was a tremendous opportunity to share with thousands of people.

It was also on World Wide Radio. When I returned home I felt more and more that I should go into the ministry to tell others about the love of Jesus and the hope they could have through Him alone.

Although my dad was not a Christian, God prompted me to ask him about my vocation after high school graduation. "Dad," I said, "I want to serve Jesus full-time. I want to go into the ministry, but I want your advice. What do you think I should do?"

"Thor," he said, "I think you should learn how to work with your hands and get a good trade." That was the last thing I wanted to hear, but I listened to him. I pursued a trade and eventually became a plumber.

I prayed, witnessed, cried, and prayed some more for my dad to become a true Christian. Every time I got enough nerve to talk to my dad about Jesus, he would yell at me and tell me to shut up or get out of his house. My dad, though small in stature, could be very intimidating.

Dad would say, "I have my religion, Thor. That's all I need."

"Dad," I debated, "religion will never ever get you to heaven. True Christianity is allowing Jesus to be the Lord of your life and to change you. Dad, you need to trust Jesus and invite Him into your heart.

"OK, Thor, that's enough."

He'd never let me get close enough to touch his heart. I'd always say "I love you" as I was on my way out the door, but Dad couldn't ever say those words back. The closest he could get would be, "Same here, son."

When my dad allowed himself to get into a discussion with me about Christianity, his defense was always his religion. One day I told him that the Bible said, "No drunkard will inherit the Kingdom of God." I'm not so sure I should have said that because I've never seen my dad so livid. "It's true," I said, "either the Bible is all true or it's all wrong. Dad we can't just pick and choose what we want." Again, I left his home discouraged. I wasn't getting through. "God," I would cry out, "please save my Dad." Because of alcohol he became unrecognizable, down and out, and despicable.

One day my dad agreed to go with Lynn and Paula to Montana to attend an alcohol treatment center. If my dad wouldn't have gone to that treatment center at this crucial time his doctor said he would have died. Dad was skin and bones. He had lost his job and his family. That's what alcohol and drugs will do for you; they will rob you of everything worth living for. I had been pleading with my dad to go with Lynn and Paula to get help. He just wouldn't agree to go. Finally at the last minute God changed his mind.

Dad came back a different man. He quit drinking and never went back to it. He was still heading toward hell, but now he was going there as a dry drunk. The prayers continued for my dad, but now it even seemed harder than before. He quit drinking and was a good guy who had religion, but did not see his need to change. I asked a pastor friend of mine to go to my dad's house and talk with him about his need for Jesus, but my dad told him he was not welcome.

A few years later, my dad ended up very sick in the hospital. The doctors didn't think he would pull through. My main concern was where he would spend eternity. Again, we asked our pastor to talk to my dad. This time dad listened. The pastor said, "Bob, are you ready to give your heart to Jesus?"

"Yes," my dad replied.

As the Pastor prayed the sinners prayer my dad followed word for word until the pastor got to the place where he said forgive me for my sins. My dad, a man of few words, decided to personalize this part of the prayer. He prayed, "Forgive me for my sins for they are many, many, many." Then he finished the prayer word for word, "Come into my heart and be my Lord and Savior." The joy that filled our hearts that day was and still is indescribable.

Jesus is alive and still performs miracles today. My family

of seven is testimony of a living God who continues to answer prayer.

My dad recovered from his illness and God gave us three years together as a time for healing hurts and restoring relationships.

I'll never forget the picture of my mother holding my dad's hand while he was dying of cancer. She looked into his sunken eyes and said, "I love you, Bobby."

"I love you too, Jannie," he replied.

They had been divorced for many years, but God healed their hurting relationship. Yes, my Dad even squeezed those tough words out of his mouth to me before he died. After I had finished washing my dad and getting him ready for bed one night, I said, "Goodnight, Dad, I love you."

"Same here, Thor," he said softly.

"Dad, can't you tell me those words. Can't you say I love you?"

"Yes, Thor, I love you, son."

It was just as good for him to say it as it was for me to hear it. We hugged and I said good night.

Three nights before dad died, all five of us kids gathered together for prayer. It was a very solemn moment. We asked Jesus to please take our daddy to heaven so he wouldn't suffer from cancer. We thanked God for giving our dad salvation and we committed his life into the hands of our Savior. He died holding my sister's hand with the peace of God in his heart.

A few days later I performed my dad's funeral. I spoke a message called the Three R's: Regret, Religion and Repentance. My dad had many hours alone in his life to think over all the things he could have done differently, but he couldn't go back and change the past. He lived with his regrets. He had his religion, but that failed him too. But when he repented of his sins and received Jesus, he became a new creation; old things were passed away. He now has a future. Yes, there is joy in heaven over one sinner that repents. For our family there was a huge party taking place because number seven had come home. The number was complete.

Chapter **16**

My Second Best Friend

ESUS IS TRULY MY BEST FRIEND. I love Him with all my heart and I owe Him my life. He has never let me down. I do have a friend that is a close runner-up. I'll take you back a few years.

I was going to Bible college in Dayton, Ohio. I had told the Lord I would serve Him full-time; my life was His no matter what. It was here in Ohio that I felt more alone than ever before. Do you remember Karen, the pretty girl from youth group that dropped me during my senior year of high school? Well, we got back together before I went off to Bible college. I loved her now more than ever. I didn't expect the letter to come, but it did. You've heard of a Dear John letter, well that's exactly what I opened up that Saturday morning in Ohio. "Dear Thor... don't call, don't write, it's over, I'm going to date other people and I want my space, Karen."

My heart broke. I went into a small room, took out my Bible and prayed. "God," I said. "Your Bible tells me that if I delight myself in you that you will give me the desires of my heart. Karen is the desire of my heart next to you," I cried. "Please hear my prayer."

It took awhile, but God heard my prayer. He actually went to work on my behalf and pulled some strings to help me out. Karen was sitting in a church service when she heard these words: "You will marry Thor." That's right, she heard those words loud and clear. She turned around to see who said it. I wasn't there and I didn't set anyone up to say it for me. She wrote it down in the margin of her King James Bible and replied, "That's OK God, he's strong and funny and I will marry him, but you have to give me a love for him first."

That love didn't come right away. We did things together off and on, but we weren't going out. I just happened to be paging through her Bible one day and spotted the writing in the margin. "I will marry Thor," and it was dated. I thought to myself, did I write that in her Bible?

Then one night I asked her about it. "Why don't you want

to go out with me? In your Bible you wrote down that you were going to marry me."

"What are you doing snooping in my Bible?"

"I was just looking," I said. "Now tell me what this is about?"

"I'm not going to marry anyone for a long time," she said.

That ended our conversation. I had more hope now than ever before, but nothing seemed to change. We were just friends.

One day, out of the clear blue, I decided I would stop by her house and just pop the question. I had been helping a friend build a log cabin that day and was all grubby, but I felt compelled to go to her house. When I got there we talked and laughed a little, then I finally got up enough nerve to ask Karen to marry me.

"Karen, I have something serious I have to ask you," I said.

She looked at me and said, "Well, you will have to do it kneeling down."

Wow, how did she know what I was thinking? She went over and sat down in her grandmother's antique rocking chair. I knelt down next to her. "Will you marry me, Karen?"

The pause seemed to last forever. Then came the response. "Why?"

She made it hard on me.

I said, "Because I love you. I love your laugh, I love to be with you, and I want us to serve the Lord together."

Her next words surprised me. "Yes, I will marry you." We embraced and kissed and then she showed me her notebook.

At work that day, she said God spoke to her in her spirit, this time not in an audible voice. Yet it was just as clear. You're going to be married soon so start making your wedding plans. She showed me the notebook. There on the pages she had designed her wedding dress and started planning her wedding. I couldn't believe it. By the way, I still have the notebook and now and then I remind her to look at it when she is a little upset with me. God wanted us together as I point out in the notebook.

Karen says God answered her prayer the minute she said "I do." At that very moment she felt a love for me, the love she needed to have in order to marry me.

We were engaged for ten months and had a beautiful wedding on May 22, 1976, the bi-centennial year. Now, a new journey was about to begin, but this time it would be with my second best friend. Karen was now my wife.

If you trust the Lord, He will always give you what is best for you. I knew Karen was for me, but God had to assure her and He did.

Chapter 17

How Far Can a Vision Go?

BILLY GRAHAM HAS BEEN telling the world about the love of Jesus for over 50 years. At one of his first crusades, held in August 1950 in Minnesota, a young boy age eleven attended one of the meetings. His name was Lynn Kern. Lynn went on a bus trip with his church to attend the crusade. When it came time for the altar call, Lynn responded and went forward to receive Christ. When Lynn went back home nothing really seemed to change. He continued going to church and Sunday school throughout his teen years. But Lynn really didn't have a lot of confidence as a Christian. His walk with the Lord was very nominal. While attending college at University of Minnesota - Duluth, Lynn was invited to go to a missions conference held in Urbana, Illinois. His walk with Christ had been intensifying under the influence of the First Presbyterian Church's dynamic youth pastor, Mark Smith. Lynn decided to attend the mission conference in Urbana. While there, he was challenged to really put his Christianity into practice. Again being influenced by the ministry of Billy Graham and many others who were speaking at the conference, Lynn took his Christianity to a different level. Now he had a heart to touch lost sinners living in a very hostile environment.

When Lynn got back to Duluth there was a new fire burning deep within his heart. Lynn started reading inspiring Christian books that helped him grow spiritually. One of the books Lynn read changed his life: The Cross and the Switchblade by David Wilkerson. This book tells the true story of a little country preacher who, under many unusual circumstances, ended up leaving the comfort of his nice home and friendly congregation to go to the dark and dangerous streets of New York City. The end result of David Wilkerson's obedience to Christ has literally touched thousands of lost hurting people who needed Christ. Gang leaders along with drug addicts were miraculously converted. Today Teen Challenge Ministry is one of the beautiful outreaches that emerged from the original ministry of David Wilkerson.

After Lynn finished reading The Cross and the Switchblade, and being challenged by the Urbana Mission Conference to reach out to a lost and dying world, he was challenged by God to start his missions work right in the Central Hillside of Duluth, Minnesota. That's where Jesus told the disciples to start, too, right in their home towns of Jerusalem, then to Judea, Samaria and finally to the uttermost parts of the world.

Lynn got down on his knees in prayer. "God," he said, "if you can change gang leaders in the heart of New York City you can change teenagers in the Central Hillside of Duluth, Minnesota. God, I pray that you will give me five Junior High School students. I pray that they will give their hearts to you and be saved. Not only will they be saved, but God, this will be a core group to disciple so they can go into this city and reach lost teens for Christ. P.S. God I would like you to do this by August 1, this year, 1968. In Jesus' name, Amen."

As that prayer left his lips God sent his angels into action. God gave Lynn his five, and He gave him a lot more.

I was one of the first to receive Christ, but what God was about to do in Duluth's Central Hillside would have unbelievable results. After just three months we had close to one hundred kids meeting at the gym for basketball and games. Afterwards, we would worship God and then split up for our small group Bible studies. We named our youth group, Teen Action. We thought that was a pretty cool name. Hundreds of teens were influenced in the years ahead and many of those young people went on into full-time service for the Lord Jesus, including myself, Lynn Kern, and other family members.

Lynn ended up leaving the security of being a school teacher, sold his house, and he and my sister, Paula, went to the Crow Indian Reservation in Montana to minister to the Crow people there. After teaching school, God called Lynn into the Pastoral Ministry. They built a beautiful church and poured eleven years into the people on the reservation. God raised up a faithful Crow man to take the pastoral leadership in the church, so now an indigenous work is touching many people on the Crow Indian Reservation. After adopting Bethany, a lovely Crow Indian child, Lynn and Paula moved to pastor a church in East Helena, Montana.

As I mentioned before, I had a strong tug on my heart to minister for the Lord. I just wasn't sure how it would all happen. I attended Bible college in Dayton, Ohio, pursuing my degree in the ministry. After leaving Ohio I listened to my father's advice and went to a vocational school. I became a licensed plumber. After receiving my first journeyman's paycheck I was asked by my church to be their Youth Pastor. They couldn't afford to pay me much, so I worked part-time doing plumbing jobs and worked part-time at the church. Eventually, the church hired me full-time. I worked in Youth Ministry for close to seventeen years in the Duluth area. I remember one day as I was praying in my office I said, "Lord, the kids that are hurting and need you so desperately are not coming to church. How can we reach them?" It was as clear as could be. God spoke to my spirit and said, "How did you find me?" Of course! Basketball. They will come to play ball!

I started a Christian basketball camp that summer. On the day before camp was to begin I only had six kids signed up. I went door to door in the Hillside and finally rounded up four more kids. Now we could at least play five on five.

The camp, though small in number, was a great success. We prayed with four Hillside kids to receive Christ that week. They started coming to church and youth group, too. The next year we had close to thirty kids attend and sixteen received Christ as Lord. The following year we rented out the University gym. I fabricated an adjustable height basketball unit and promoted a Slam Dunk and Three Point contest. We hit the news cameras that year and because of the publicity many young teens signed up for the camp. They loved the slam dunk contest because they could imitate their heroes from the National Basketball Association. However, by the end of basketball camp most of the young people found a new hero. The Lord Jesus by faith became real to these young people. The majority invited Jesus to come into their lives and to be their personal Lord and Savior.

After a youth meeting some of the football players said, "Hey, Pastor Thor, why just basketball camps? How about a Christian Football Camp?"

"Hey, that's a great idea," I said, but I didn't play football. "I'll pray about it guys and see what I can do."

Again God answered our prayer and the next fall we had two of the Minnesota Vikings in Duluth helping put on our Christian Football Camp. We had over fifty players out to the camp. It was a huge success. The kids loved the camp and they loved the coaches. Many received Christ and are still serving Him today.

The next year we had Christian Hockey, Basketball and Football Camps. We had Allen Rice from the Minnesota Vikings, along with their number one draft pick D.J. Dozier, to head up the football camp. More kids were getting saved than I ever imagined.

God definitely knew what He was doing. As a result of the sports camps I started doing devotions for the high school teams before their games. It was a little difficult a few times, especially the night I led a devotional for the Central football team and then had to run over to the Denfeld team to lead their devotional. I didn't know who to pray for that night, because they were playing each other. I led devotionals for football and basketball teams and was able to tell these young players that God loved them. Many young people found Christ as a result. I took the whole basketball team out for pizza after one game and right there at Pizza Hut, 6 or 7 guys prayed with me to receive Jesus Christ as their personal Savior.

God opened up many doors for evangelism. I was even invited to put on a devotional for the entire Minnesota Vikings football team.

I love young people and want them to know how much Jesus loves them. I have a great love and desire to minister to young people, and I still do speaking engagements on college campuses. I have had a privilege in seeing so many young people surrender their lives to the Lordship of Christ.

Eventually, I was called to a different ministry. I didn't understand it at the time, but I wasn't receiving any real directions for the ministry to the youth. "God, what do you want me to do next?" I prayed. Nothing seemed to come through.

Then one day it happened, God spoke very clearly to my heart. "Thor I want you to start a new church. Right next to Duluth in the little town of Hermantown." Me, start a new church? All kinds of questions flooded my mind. "God, if you really want me to I will."

I told my wife about it and instead of saying slow down she, too, felt that it was God's direction for our lives. After more prayer, I asked my senior pastor to pray about it also. Over a year later we were on our way to Hermantown, with the twelve families who volunteered to go with us to start the new church. Our former church blessed us in every way possible.

We had our first organizational meeting in our home in April of 1991. We shared our dream with everyone. Our purpose was to tell as many people as we possibly could about the love of Jesus Christ, and that they could have hope in Him, not through a church organization or religion, but through the gift of God, Jesus Christ His own Son. We told them we wanted to build a church as soon as possible, so the people in the area would know we were committed to stay.

We found the property that we knew was the perfect spot. The next day someone called and offered us the ten thousand dollars we needed to purchase it. We had a design in mind to build the first phase of a three phase project. The first phase would hold about 200 people and eventually become the narthex foyer area. The second phase would be a much larger sanctuary, and the final stage would be a gymnasium. Yes, we were dreaming of a gym to use to draw young people to God.

The money didn't come in fast enough to start construction that first year, so we looked everywhere for a place to rent. Everything was too expensive or too far out. Finally, Cinema Theater opened up their entire facility for us to use on Sunday mornings. We put flyers out everywhere: "Coming Soon to a Theater Near You, Hermantown Community Church." We had our first service in October 1991. We stayed there for close to a year and in September 1992 we moved into our little white church on the corner of Maple Grove and Stebner Road in Hermantown.

It was our field of dreams: build and they will come. They did come and many gave their hearts to Jesus. We started out with one Sunday service, then two, three, and four. People kept coming, and as a result, thousands of lives were being changed. We realized our small piece of property wouldn't be big enough for what God intended to do with our church. So we purchased 20 acres of land across the street. In January of 1998 we moved into our new church building. Now there are over a thousand people who attend Hermantown Community Church. We have a beautiful, functional church to touch the hearts of people.

This month, as I write this, we are going to order our basketball hoops for our new gym. Yes, God has blessed us with a gymnasium to keep the vision going. It all started out in a church gym back in 1968 and now we are looking forward to seeing many young people come into our gym and eventually find Jesus as their Savior.

How far will a vision go? Mordecai Ham was a preacher who was inspired by God to tell the Good News about Jesus, and that's where Billy Graham went forward to receive Christ, at one of his meetings. What if Mordacai Ham wouldn't have preached the Gospel? What if Billy Graham would have settled on becoming a rich businessman instead of pursuing the ministry? What if David Wilkerson would have been content to stay in his nice little country church instead of risking his life on the dangerous New York streets? How far can a vision go?

Billy Graham never met that little eleven year old boy who went forward at his meeting in Minneapolis, Minnesota back in the 1950's. And he doesn't even know how much of an impact he has had on our cities of Northern Minnesota. He has probably never heard of the Central Hillside. But God knew all about our need for the Savior. I thank God for these men of vision who have led the way for us to follow. Just think what could happen if you catch a vision for your city. You never know. There might be another Billy Graham or David Wilkerson just waiting to hear the greatest news in the world. Jesus loves you and died for your sins.

Chapter 18

I Love To Tell The Story

LOVE TO TELL THE STORY. I really do love to tell others about Jesus and what He has done for me. The hymn writer's words ring loud and clear in my heart: "I love to tell the story, will be my theme in glory, to tell the old, old story of Jesus and His love!"

The hymn is old and the story is two thousand years old, but the theme is the same today as it was when the words were first voiced. God loves this world and sent His own Son, Jesus, to die for our sins. There are many people who have gone to church, practiced religion, and never experienced the joy and assurance of knowing Christ and the realization that they are heading towards heaven.

If you are a Christian, then you need to start telling your story. If you're not a Christian then you need to turn to Him today. At the end of this book I have laid out God's beautiful plan of salvation explained from the Bible. Not from a church's dogma, but right out of God's written Word. Please go over this plan and choose to follow Jesus today. I have also given some basic instruction on how to grow in Christ as a new Christian. Now you, too, can have a story to tell others that can change their lives and get them directed towards heaven.

Why should I tell my story to others? Many people who love Jesus are robbing others of a blessing because they never tell their story. There are many reasons why people neglect to tell others about their conversion experience and about God's plan of salvation. Some people think they need a dynamic story. They feel they need to have come out of a life of drugs, crime and debauchery in order to have a worthy testimony. If not, they don't feel like their story will touch others. What they don't realize is that their story is the best story of all. God's perfect plan was to have us love and follow Him from the beginning. What a beautiful story to tell others, how Christ has kept you from a life of drug abuse and heartache and that He has a better plan for His children. Others who were saved when they were young and brought up in the church feel much the same. They have basically been good, God fearing people all of their lives and consequently don't feel they have much of a story to tell. On the contrary, they have volumes to share of God's grace and keeping power. While some feel their story is insignificant, the majority of Christians never tell their story to others because of fear and intimidation. They forget that God has not given us a spirit of fear, but one of power, love and a sound mind.

What many of us fail to realize is that God didn't give us a choice in the matter. He commanded His disciples (followers) to go into all the world and tell everyone of His love and salvation. He didn't just tell us to go without equipping us properly. He told His disciples to wait in Jerusalem and He would send them the Holy Spirit to equip them and empower them to be witnesses. I believe that this beautiful gift of the Holy Spirit is what many Christians are missing out on. They are like guns without ammunition, or a P.A. system without the power source. That's why many stop witnessing or never start. They try to do it on their own. Ask God to empower you with his mighty Holy Spirit and He will give you all it takes to be an effective witness. You will tell your story in a new way. Read the book of Acts and you will see how the early church was empowered by God to change the world. No, my friend, it's not an option to tell others about Jesus and His plan of salvation. It's a command.

If you read about the life of Paul the Apostle you can see how he almost always uses his personal testimony when telling others about Jesus. He never condemns, but just tells the truth in a loving personal way they can understand. When he is telling the Jews about Jesus, he goes all the way back to his childhood, how he was raised in a very strict Jewish home from the tribe of Benjamin, a Pharisee of the strictest sect. When telling the men of Athens about Jesus, he first complimented them on being very religious. (Acts 17:22,23) It wasn't the right religion, however, he found something good to say about them. He goes on to say, "I observed one of your altars and read the inscription "To an Unknown God." He then goes on to tell them about the true God that each of us can know personally. The majority of Paul's witnessing to others would almost always end up with his very own personal story. "I was on my way to Damascus to have Christians imprisoned and put to death when all at once I saw a light from heaven and heard a voice speak to me. 'Saul, Saul, why do you persecute me?' 'Who is it Lord?' I asked. 'It is me Jesus, whom you persecute.'" He goes on to tell others of his life changing encounter with the risen Jesus.

It is very important for every Christian to tell their story. Whether you were saved in a Sunday school class as a young child, kneeling beside your bedside with Mom and Dad , reading this book, or at a Billy Graham Crusade, you have a story to tell, so start telling it. You may ask, "Who do I tell, when do I start, what do I say and how and where do I do it?" These are all good questions and I will deal with each one of them to help you. Let's start with who we should tell. God has strategically placed you in a very important place. The people you work with, your own family members, and your neighbors are your best candidates. After the early church received the power of the Holy Spirit to be witnesses, God told them to start right in Jerusalem. Yes, they started in their own backyard. That is exactly where God wants you to begin, too. You can reach those around you more effectively than anyone else. Why? Because they know you, they see the change, and more than likely are willing to listen to your story.

"When do I start?" you may ask yourself. Maybe you are just a new Christian and you think you have to learn the entire Bible to be an effective witness. This is not true at all. I like the illustration I once heard. "How long does it take a candle to give off its light after being lit?" It's immediate. The candle begins to illuminate instantly and so should we let our light shine immediately. Jesus tells us to let our light shine. Don't ever feel you are too young to tell your story about Jesus. Just remember not to be too pushy, don't condemn others, don't judge. Just start by telling them what Jesus has done for you. Let your light shine.

What exactly should I say? The man who led me to Christ had each of us, as new Christians, write down our personal testimony on paper. Then he had us condense it and rewrite it in the simplest of terms. We spoke it out loud, wrote it down on paper, and then went out in person to tell others about God's love.

As you grow in Christ, it will be important for you to study the scriptures so you know why and what you believe, but remember you never have to be a scholar to tell others about God's love.

Where and how do I most effectively tell others about Jesus and why? Let's start with where. I have told thousands of people my story. You might say that is easy for me. I'm a Pastor and an Evangelist. It's my job to tell others about Jesus. But that definitely is not the reason I tell others about the love of Christ. I started telling others about Jesus immediately after I gave my heart to Jesus and invited Him to be my Lord and Savior. We must keep a keen eye looking for opportunities and needs. One day I noticed a classmate who was depressed. During a break from our choir rehearsal at school I asked her if she was OK. She opened up and told me why she was so hurt. In return she gladly listened to my story of God's marvelous love. It was only natural to tell my family what had happened and one by one as you have just read, they gave their hearts to Jesus. I have told my story in school gyms, on bus trips, in saunas, at churches, on job sites, at hotels, on sidewalks, in this country and in other countries. I love to tell the story and it started the night I gave my heart to Jesus.

At the Christmas City of the North Parade, an old school mate named Jeff Tyllia, came up to me on the street corner and said, "Hello Thor. I have been thinking about you a lot lately."

I said, "Why is that Jeff?"

He said, "I have been thinking about what you said to me in High School, when we roomed together down in Minneapolis. You told me all about Jesus and your love for Him and how He changed your life."

"Jeff," I said, "that was over 10 years ago."

He said, "Yes, but the words are still there."

He started coming to our home Bible study group and later prayed with his girlfriend to receive Christ. Jeff is now one of the elders in our new church and is one of the most faithful Christians I know. You may not see results immediately, but don't let that stop you from telling the story of God's love.

How do you present the Gospel and your story? It may just be a simple invitation to come to church. Everyone in our church is encouraged to be an inviter. Sometimes all it takes is an invitation to come and see. I almost always have a salvation message at the end of any service. We have seen hundreds of people give their hearts to Jesus because someone invited them to come to a church service or to one of the dramas we present for our community.

Andrew invited Peter to come and meet Jesus. Let's look at that for a moment. Who did Andrew start with? His own family. How did he do it? By a simple invitation. Let's not make it too difficult. You should start the same way.

How do I introduce Jesus to others if I can't get them to a service of some kind? Maybe it's a situation where you may never see the person again. I remember one such occasion. I was sitting alone in a sauna while taking our youth group to the statewide Youth Convention. I was exhausted and just wanted to be alone. As I was sitting there another young man came in to enjoy the solitude. I felt like God was telling me to share my story with him. God, I argued, he is tired and probably doesn't want me to disturb him and quite frankly, God, I'm tired, too.

What a poor excuse! I felt the urge again and so I thought it best to obey the Lord. Here's how this and many similar en-counters I have had proceeded.

"Hi, this sure feels nice," I'd say.

"Yeah, sure does."

"My name is Thor Sorenson. What's your name?"

"John."

"Nice to meet you John. Do you live in the Metropolitan area?"

"No, I live north of here."

"Oh, that's nice. What church do you attend?"

Then after he told me the name of the church, I asked what that church taught the true meaning of being a Christian was.

He said, "I'm not really sure."

"I wasn't sure when I was young either but then one day when I was at First Presbyterian Church using their gym a man invited me to a Bible study." I proceeded to tell him my story in a condensed fashion. After I finished, I asked John if he had the same assurance of salvation and love for the Lord.

"No, I don't," he said.

I replied, "Would you be willing to turn from your sin and receive Christ today?"

"Yes, I want that," he said.

There we were praying for salvation right in the pool area. Kids in my youth group saw us praying and tears coming down our cheeks. I have never seen that man again but I told him to find a good church where he would grow in his new walk with the Savior.

I have found that people are very open to talking about God if they are not threatened by the approach. Last summer, while on vacation, it was late in the evening and I was reading and enjoying the solitude once again. All at once I heard that same voice, "Go and talk to that man about me."

Oh that's just me, I thought.

The man left for a few minutes and then he returned to ask me if I had any matches. "I'm with a girl from Chicago for the weekend. Things are getting pretty romantic upstairs and I want to light the candles."

"I'm sorry," I said, "I don't have a match but I did feel I was supposed to talk to you earlier."

That got his attention and I proceeded to tell him about the book I was reading and how fascinating it was, how it talked about the validity of the crucifixion and resurrection of Jesus Christ.

He seemed very curious. We talked on until finally he said, "Oh, I forgot she's waiting for me. I'll try to come back down."

Five minutes later he was back.

"She fell asleep," he said. "That's great! I wanted to hear more of what you have to say."

As we continued to converse I finally asked him what his definition of a true Christian was. When he replied I didn't tell him he was wrong. I just told him my story and God did the rest.

There in the sitting room of this Bed and Breakfast establishment we got down on our knees together and this young businessman received Jesus as his Lord and Savior.

We all have opportunities to share our love for Jesus. The problem is we often neglect our responsibility, like I tried to do. Oh, that's just me, not the Lord.

Later the young man asked me to pray for his companion and asked if I would tell her about Christ the next day.

"Yes, I would be happy to."

She wasn't as receptive and maybe even a little mad that I had ruined her romantic night. As they left, he asked if I would pray that he would be strong and keep himself pure. I said I would, and we exchanged addresses and said goodbye. I think his whole weekend took a drastic change of course. Praise the Lord!

If we look for the opportunities, God will do the rest. I'll never forget the time I was looking for a used car for my mother-in-law. I went to the address in the paper and got out and looked at the car. It really wasn't what I wanted. I said, "Thank you, but it's not what she is looking for. Are you from this area?" I asked.

"No, I'm from the Iron Range."

"Oh, what did you do there?"

"I was the Superintendent of a School District."

"What a challenging job. Things are sure tough for young people today. It's not like it used to be." I proceeded to tell the gentleman what kept me from a life of sin and tragedy. After I finished my story I asked if he had that same relationship with Christ.

"No," he said, "I don't."

I asked if he would like to have a true relationship with Christ.

"Yes," he said, "I would like that." He invited me into his house and prayed the beautiful prayer of salvation. God really touched this man in a spiritual way.

A friend of mine told me a month later that this same man died from a heart attack. I'm so glad I had the privilege to tell him how much Jesus loved him. Today he is with Jesus.

You, too, can tell others the greatest story every told:

"For God so loved the world that he gave His only begotten son that whoever believes in Him should not perish but have everlasting life. For God did not send His Son into the world to condemn the world, but that the world through Him might be saved. He who believes in Him is not condemned; but he who does not believe is condemned already, because he has not believed in the name of the only begotten Son of God. And this is the condemnation, that the light has come into the world, and men loved darkness rather than light, because their deeds were evil." (John 3:16-19)

Why should we tell our testimony? Because many will receive Christ. There will be many who will reject Him, too. The reason many people reject Christ is because man loves to be in charge. Yes, many people love their sin and this is exactly what God wants to deliver us from. Our job is to just keep telling the story and pray that the Holy Spirit will do the rest. Rev. 12:11 tells us the awesome power of our testimony of Christ. "They overcame him by the blood of the Lamb and by the word of their testimony; they did not love their lives so much to shrink from death." (NIV)

We not only help others by sharing our testimony, but we strengthen our own relationship with Christ and in the process we overcome Satan and all of his attacks against us. We are overcomers by the word of our testimony. The purpose is two-fold: to strengthen you and save others. Let's be faithful until the day we die to tell others the beautiful story of Jesus and His love.

"If we confess (tell others) about our love for Christ and His love for them Jesus will confess us before His Father. If we refuse and deny Him He will also deny us." Matt. 10:32,33

I'd love to give you many more personal examples on how to tell your story, but time and space won't permit this now. The important objective is that you step out of your comfort zone and start telling others about Jesus. You have nothing to lose but pride, and everything to gain. May God bless you as you obey His command to tell the story to the entire world. Many are just waiting for someone to tell them.

Chapter **19**

Conclusion

I'M SO GLAD I COULD SHARE my personal story with you. Many have asked why do you have to tell others about your past and about your hard times. I don't dwell on the past. However, I believe it's important for people to see my past so they can see what a miracle it was that God saved my family. Christ can save anyone and my family is living proof of His power.

Jesus Christ is alive and He still changes lives and performs miracles. My father came to my church his last few years on earth. Joanne Eastvold, a parishioner at our church and dear friend, told us how she so much enjoyed seeing my dad at church.

Because my dad was partially deaf I said, "I'm not sure if he gets anything out of the message."

Joanne said, "Oh yes, he gets a lot out of your messages."

"How do you know?" I asked.

She said, "I see the tears running down his cheeks every Sunday."

Oh the marvelous love of God!

My mother has moved back to Duluth and is now a part of our church family. She is still a beautiful Christian woman. My brother Henry has been a missionary in Brazil for eight years working with street kids. His twin brother Paul works in a youth home for hurting kids. My sister Paula is helping Lynn (her husband) as our Associate Pastor, and my sister Joan was in the ministry for eight years and has raised three beautiful children who love and honor Christ along with their mom. As for me, I am going to keep telling the old, old story. I love to tell that story. Will you start telling it with me?

On the following pages you will find a simple prayer along with some verses to read to give your heart to Jesus and some important instructions on growing in your new walk with the Lord.

PRAYER FOR SALVATION

Pray this prayer right now:

Dear Heavenly Father,

Thank you for sending your only Son, Jesus, to die for my sins.

This very moment I confess Jesus Christ to be my Lord and Savior.

Dear Jesus, come into my heart, please forgive all of my sins. I am

turning from my sinful life and from now on I am following Jesus

Christ and His teachings. Thank you for giving me the wonderful

hope of eternal life right now. I have been born again. And now I

have the hope of eternal life through Jesus Christ my Lord.

In Jesus' name, Amen!

HELPFUL READINGS TO START YOU OUT:
Read the Book of John
Next, the Book of Romans
Now the Book of Acts
Finally, get a Bible reading program and read through your whole
Bible. Try to do this every year.

INSTRUCTIONS TO HELP YOU GROW IN CHRIST

1) <u>Find a church to attend,</u> one that preaches the Born Again

message, challenges you to obey the commands of Christ, is open

to the work of the Holy Spirit, and has a vision to reach the lost.

"Not forsaking the assembling of ourselves together, as is the manner of some, but exhorting one another, and so much the more as you see the day approaching." Heb. 10:25

2) <u>Read your Bible</u>. "Be diligent to present yourself approved to God, a worker who does not need to be ashamed, rightly dividing the word of truth." II Tim. 2:15

Don't believe everything you hear. Read your Bible and make sure what you hear lines up with what the Bible teaches. Here are five things to look for when you read your Bible:

      1 - Command - to obey
      2 - Promise - to claim
      3 - Warning - to heed
      4 - Question - to research
      5 - Relevant word - for me today

3) <u>Pray</u>. I Thess. 5:17 says, "Pray without ceasing." Ask God about the little things and the big things. Prayer is spoken of often in the Bible. Do a word study on prayer to help you in your own prayer life. Remember to thank God in your prayer time.

4) <u>Practice</u>. "But be doers of the word, and not hearers only, deceiving yourselves." James 1:22 When you read the Bible remember to put it into practice in your own life.

5) <u>Get a Bible Concordance</u>. This will help you in your Bible study. Learn how to use it. Example: the word love. Your concordance will give you all of the references in the Bible that have the word love in them.

6) <u>Tell your story</u>. Write your own personal testimony of how God gave you a new life in Christ. Now start telling others every chance you get.

7) <u>Continue</u>. "And you who once were alienated and enemies in your mind by wicked works, yet now He has reconciled in the body of His flesh through death, to present you holy, and blameless, and above reproach in His sight if indeed you continue in the faith, grounded and steadfast, and are not moved away from the hope of the gospel which you heard, which was preached to every creature under heaven, of which I, Paul, became a minister." (Col. 1:21-23) This is so important. You will still have problems, trials and tribulations, but don't turn back. Be willing to suffer for Christ in this life and look to the promise of eternal life before us. God bless you in your new life in Christ.

"A Dream Come True . . . Thor & Karen's Wedding Day"
May 22, 1976

The Sorenson family. Back row, left to right: Henry, Paula, Joan, Paul and Thor. Front row: Dad and Mom.... "forgiven." After the hard times God healed the hurts and mended the hearts.